“A child’s name is its most important part.”

- anonymous

BETTER NAMES
(for baby)

Charles Vestal & Matt Sorrell

Written and designed in Brooklyn, NY

www.betternamesforbaby.com
betternames@betternamesforbaby.com

ISBN 978-0-557-95663-0

"A rose by any other name would smell as sweet."

- Wyllyym Schokksparr

Introduction

Inside these pages, you will find classics mixed with the unconventional. Indeed, you may find a label you might not wish upon yourself. But rejoice, for today, you name another. For a child, a name can be a source of power and courage, or a way to define one's self in the world and chart a course for one's own life. But do we not wish our children could live in the days of discovery, of Columbus, Magellan and Pizarro, discovering what once was new? Deny them their maps, and let a child sail alone.

A unique moniker is the new parent's first hurdle. The first words a child hears are his or her own name. Why give him the same footing as every Thomnm, Tdyck or Thahri?

Choose a unique incantation to usher him into this life. Failure in the beginning is not an option. Standing out from the crowd is the best chance your child has in this world. Names' popularities wane and wax–a longer last than any fame or praise is that of obscurity and shame.

Many parents opt to give their child a middle name, as an alternative, or family remembrance. We feel every newborn should have, at a minimum, three spare names, in case of emergency or flight of fancy. Keep these auxiliary names in a sealed envelope, but in a spot that the child might stumble upon. A closed, but not taped, cigar box would work splendidly. Cigars may remain, if desired.

Enjoy all and please add a check mark next to those you use.

Names

h

Ahpt

Airor

Akce

Akerp

Akk

Akses

Allob

Allstitch

Anda

Anfarloin

Anip

Ank

Anklor

Anned

Arkord

Asdar

Ashhhh

Ask

Askat

Asker

Astroyd

Aybee

Badg

Baggey

Bahmil

Banded

Barrell

Basoline

Baybley

Beerd

Beraz

Bernerd

Berque

Bewt

Bhuurp

Billiam

Billip

Bilune

Bin

Biss

Blaf

Blick

Boass

Bock

Boney

Bongly

Bont

Bonzleby

Booj

Booton

Bottem

Bowled

Bowwe

Boyle

Boyng

Brand

Brarby

Brart

Bred

Breendle

Bremp

Brerp

Bringo

Brisaley

Brisque

Brive

Brj

Brolish

Brownerd

Brownish

Brozzy

Brumb

Brung

Budbull

Bulf

Bunp

Burdston

Bure

Burf

Burng

Bylamp

Bylls

Byng

Bytt

Byzzy

abbi

Caelmore

Caep

Caldroon

Calmo

Cample

Camponk

Campson

Camt

Cancel

Canthony

Canvel

Capple

Carper

Cawl

Ceebler

Ceech

Ceed

Ceedee

Ceert

Celsey

Cemibold

Centch

Central

Cert

Chamble

Chandelier

Charty

Cheet

Cheg

Chelpland

Chember

Chemp

Cheppes

Cherbert

Chimel

Chinp

Chug

Cinched

Cink

Cint

Cist

Cjemp

Clairetine

Clammet

Clammette

Clample

Claw

Claysh

Cleara

Clernk

Clinkelle

Cloor

Cloy

Cm

Conelope

Cremp

Crep

Creta

Crikt

Crump

Crunge

Crunt

Cry

Cryzz

Cuipp

Culmo

Cunch

Curnt

ack

Daereel

Davinoff

Deeb

Deek

Def

Delthany

Dent

Derrer

Dewlton

Dewq

Dgordge

Diert

Din

Dinb

Dip

Dispear

Divutte

Dixy

Dizme

Doil

Doldrum

Dorrell

Dossier

Doubleyew

Dramb

Dreg

Drilk

Drink

Drunn

Dup

Dyll

Dym

Dyme

Dyp

Dyphen

aggle

Earb

Eartle

Eenkle

Eent

Eertd

Eggle

Eighth

Eip

Elky

Elpful

Emmment

Enkle

Ensest

Epcel

Erd

Ern

Ernd

Error

Ersoms

Ertle

Eskuttle

Esssss

Ett

Eulf

Ewrikk

Ewrl

aaa

Faeink

Famb

Famil

Fammble

Fanly

Fapple

Farncy

Faymish

Faynt

Feeen

Feffle

Fellure

Fent

Fernt

Fertow

Fesar

Fest

Few

Fild

Filnette

Fing

Fint

Fipple

Firny

Fish

Flaily

Flibley

Flik

Florrr

Flosty

Fluance

Fold

Foon

Franosera

Frasse

Fratina

Fremp

Friendsy

Frint

Froong

Frunt

Fryj

Fump

Fussole

Fyg

am

Gammy

Gape

Garno

Geg

Geggert

Ghest

Ghug

Gibbler

Giblot

Glanthony

Gloin

Glosh

Gmmb

Gnimp

Gole

Golvie

Gonno

Gorge

Grabf

Grate

Gread

Grees

Grep

Grerp

Grimb

Gripple

Grist

Grosche

Growt

Grunk

Gulpole

Gurfelf

Gurfelm

Gurlb

Gursh

Guz

H

Haa'a

Halbled

Halerdgy

Happle

Harbor

Harrassa

Hassul

Heathed

Hebsin

Heed

Heeir

Heltler

Hemmer

Hert

Hhut

Hig

Hijk

Hilgish

Hillip

Hinge

Hix

Hlost

Hoarhiss

Hobiq

Hok

Hollraft

Homp

Hoop

Hore

Horsemouth

Hottel

Hube

Hurng

Hutt

Hyme

Hynje

Hyrossa

Hyt

I

Igghck

Ikkki

Ilgia

Illick

Illummy

Imron

Inion

Ink

Int

Ionnica

Irrr

J

Jakonsum

Jall

Jamb

Jeen

Jelbow

Jepond

Jerl

Jert

Jilliam

Jillip

Jingly

Jiss

Jm

Jmbb

Jmp

Joapp

Joil

Jolbo

Jook

Joynt

Jtim

Juliert

Jumbony

Jurgens

Jyn

Kambpfor

Kambron

Kanction

Kard

Karssy

Kayble

Keenov

Kelf

Kelorp

Kelper

Kelt

Kelture

Kemples

Kerm

Kettle

Kimoo

Kinge

Kizrat

Klammer

Klamp

Klandjosefine

Klarl

Klaytum

Kleblow

Klidden

Klikkle

Klip

Klonm

Kloop

Klyje

Kmblr

Koil

Krad

Krantario

Kravv

Krawly

Kujz

Kun

Kwat

Kwillent

Kyll

Lacto

Langth

Lanper

Leandeen

Leck

Leckette

Ledderd

Lelp

Lelshly

Lelslend

Lewq

Liandanne

Libidia

Liddd

Liealine

Limbre

Limilla

Limmer

Lint

Lip

Lisk

Listy

Llolly

Loader

Loim

Lonarara

Lonmir

Loom

Loopon

Loujie

Lull

Lylt

Madgic

Maep

Mairnet

Majjjjnet

Mamanda

Man

Manjoll

Mans

Markarifart

Marthur

Men

Mep

Merk

Merssessa

Mhat

Minarto

Minosse

Mitty

Mnop

Moaming

Moax

Moggl

Moil

Molko

Monkry

Monly

Mons

Morona

Moy

Moyn

Mq

Muhg

Muke

Mull

Mylar

N

Namporkette

Narf

Narr

Nekke

Nerk

Neslie

Nest

Neuto

Nimp

Nincy

Ninmpy

Nit

Nittie

Nk

No

Noazey

Nobbina

Noij

Noiman

Noodlie

Nopley

Nords

Norn

Notjohn

Nube

Nudd

Nudle

Nug

Nuldge

Nurgmarna

Nurrt

Nurt

Nyb

Nymbo

Nyme

Nyssy

Nyurny

ak

Obseese

Ocba

Occccco

Oif

Onglysh

Onk

Ooo

Oouf

Opo

Orjan

Ortp

Ouesy

P

'pip

Pakky

Palish

Pank

Panolia

Paynt

Pearson

Peeno

Pelbo

Pelg

Pelk

Pepplar

Pepta

Perkertt

Permp

Pernt

Perta

Perural

Pewn

Pewrt

Phace

Phaint

Phamil

Phayg

Phew

Piarra

Pilk

Pill

Pillard

Pilque

Pinf

Pinque

Pinte

Placenty

Plagert

Plant

Plark

Plarma

Plarty

Playt

Pleat

Plig

Plina

Plirfeck

Ploo

Plot

Ployla

Pludt

Pobby

Pogger

Poi

Poim

Pointie

Poinz

Poizenne

Pollypol

Polmo

Polot

Pols

Pompon

Pon

Ponce

Ponilly

Pontly

Poolrat

Poroon

Poz

Prank

Prarfisha

Praydio

Preg

Preiten

Prerker

Printer

Prong

Prooup

Prusha

Ptepid

Ptetpsyy

Ptom

Pucumbra

Pulmlie

Pulmran

Pulpy

Pult

Purb

Purrt

Pusch

Puster

Pwyrnte

Pynessa

Pyssy

Qant

Qeen

Qew

Qix

Qm

Qolly

Qomas

Qope

Qtx

Quaff

Quapp

Quelch

Quench

Querty

Quirt

Quoogle

Quorange

Quumble

Quypp

Raburt

Raet

Reck

Reckle

Reem

Reepond

Reet

Relb

Reldo

Remp

Renk

Rer

Rerber

Rerm

Retrow

Retsina

Retzche

Rhemb

Rhot

Rick?

Rickory

Rimley

Rinch

Rindle

Rink

Ripot

Ristle

Rit

Rocery

Roin

Roist

Roop

Root

Rown

Rrrrrick

Rudge

Rulsh

Rumma

Rumphf

Rwrynch

Saft

Sank

Sankshun

Saraan

Saringe

Sbonny

Schrank

Scribdt

Sealing

Sed

Sef

Sellery

Semical

Sewnen

Shant

Shelcure

Shellved

Shelp

Shent

Shhhell

Shiks

Shink

Shorts

Shul

Skiffer

Skrag

Skreen

Sladder

Slammi

Slank

Slara

Slarrison

Slarry

Slaw

Slax

Slig

Slint

Slit

Slurt

Smaysh

Smolerry

Snag

Sowle

Spink

Splech

Splych

Srorerer

SS

Stuv

Sumption

Susperience

Swaaron

Sweck

Swerin

Synbak

Tabe

Taffne

Taity

Tampshun

Tangeant

Tannp

Tari

Tck

Telfon

Telt

Terb

Terbleston

Terl

Terpand

Terrk

Thwara

Thynne

Tin

Tinn

Tinne

Tinnn

Tip

Tlambre

Tocp

Tramerica

Trank

Trart

Triangles

Trole

Trumpore

Trupple

Tulf

Tup

Turtie

Tweck

Tweeb

Twerd

Twind

Twrerndle

Txoxt

Tyble

Tybo

Tylt

Tyn

Tynne

Tynnq

Typ

Tyre

Tyss

i

Umblo

Ummg

Ummmblo

Undonio

V

Vagourn

Vargey

Veebond

Veese

Vellope

Venjantz

Verb

Vermia

Vest

Villy

Vilth

Voicle

Voimmy

Voodoor

Voooh

Vounous

Vulney

Vyrry

'ear

W'For

Waffor

Wahlshun

Wajks

Weeern

Weendeen

Weeper

Went

Werrick

Wert

Werth

Wet

Wets

Wetton

Whaling

Whetter

Whyne

Wobbend

Wongle

Wopple

Wowwe

Wramp

Wulsh

Wump

Wyde

Wymm

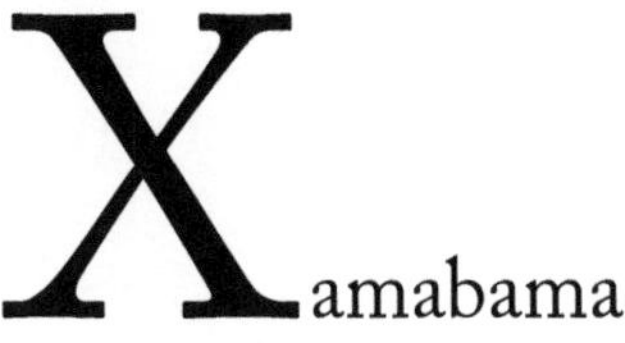

Xamabama

Xappo

Xep

Xervix

Xmeld

Xymon

Y

Yaylar

Yeaman

Yebble

Yeeled

Yeggle

Yell

Yelssy

Yerd

Yet

Yibble

Yoizle

Yonnora

Yount

Yring

Yukool

Yundle

Yunt

Yurk

Yutte

Zert

Zob

Zollipop

Zug

Zyzz

Notes:

Notes:

Notes:

Notes:

www.ingramcontent.com/pod-product-compliance
Ingram Content Group UK Ltd.
Pitfield, Milton Keynes, MK11 3LW, UK
UKHW020220250726
13967UKWH00001B/106

9 780557 956630